# Contents

Welcome 2

1 Let's explore together 4

2 Let's be happy at home 12

Review Units 1 and 2 20

3 Let's explore nature 22

4 Let's try new activities 30

Review Units 3 and 4 38

5 Let's share our food 40

6 Let's have vacation fun 48

Review Units 5 and 6 56

Goodbye 58

Celebrations 60

Picture Dictionary 62

# Welcome to the Rise and Shine Explorers Club

**1** Trace and match.

Hello, I'm Oscar.

This is Tess.

Hello, I'm Basil.

My name's Stella.

Hi, I'm Clara.

And that's Peanut.

**Tell me!**
Who is your favorite character?

**2** Read and number.

Friday ☐

Monday ☐

Thursday ☐

Saturday ☐

Wednesday ☐

Tuesday ☐

Sunday ①

Is it Monday today? Tell a friend.

**Extra time?**

**3** Find and circle. Then trace and write the number.

eleven [11]

thirteen ☐

fifteen ☐

sixteen ☐

eighteen ☐

twenty ☐

**Let's build!**
This is my pen.
It's red.

**4** (0.13) Listen and color. Then say.

1

2

3

4

**I can shine!**

**5** Trace, write, and draw for you. Then say.

Hello! I'm
_____.
This is my
_____.

color me

Say words that start with *p*.

Extra time?

# 1 Let's explore together

**Let's review!** SB p7 ➡ Find and trace. Then say.

pen · ruler · eraser

**1** Trace and number.

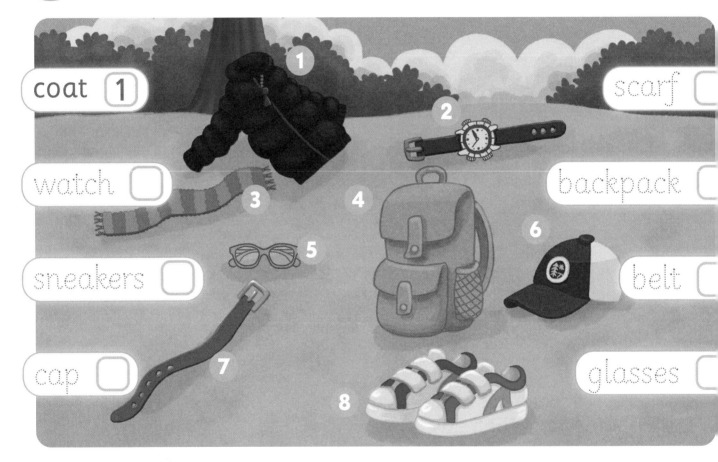

coat [1]

scarf

watch ☐

backpack ☐

sneakers ☐

belt

cap ☐

glasses

**Tell me!**

What can you put on your head? Circle.

glasses

cap

sneakers

**Extra time?** Say the words in alphabetical order.

**1**  Listen and circle.

**1**

(Yes)/ No

**2**

Yes / No

**3**

Yes / No

**4**

Yes / No

**2** Trace. Then look and circle.

Do you have…

1 sneakers?

(Yes, I do) / No, I don't.

2 a scarf?

Yes, I do. / No, I don't.

3 a belt?

Yes, I do. / No, I don't.

4 a coat?

Yes, I do. / No, I don't.

**I can shine!**

**3** Circle and color.
Then ask and answer.

Do you have
a yellow belt?

Yes, I do.

 yellowbelt

redscarf

color me

What are your favorite clothes? _____

**1** SB p12–13 ➡ **Trace. Then read and circle.**

Do you have
*glasses /
backpacks?*

Do you have a
*backpack /
mascot?*

The Explorers Club
has a *mascot /
scarf!*

**2** 🖍 **Find and color the caps. Then count and write.**

**Let's imagine!**
How many caps
do you have?

**I can shine!**

**3** ✏️ 💬 **Draw three things.
Then ask and answer.**

*Do you have
a scarf?*

*No, I don't.*

color me

Which is your favorite story frame? Why? Tell a friend.

**Extra
time?**

**1** Trace. Then look and write.

short hair ☐ **1**

long hair ☐

dark hair ☐

blond hair ☐

**2** Follow, find, and write. Then say.

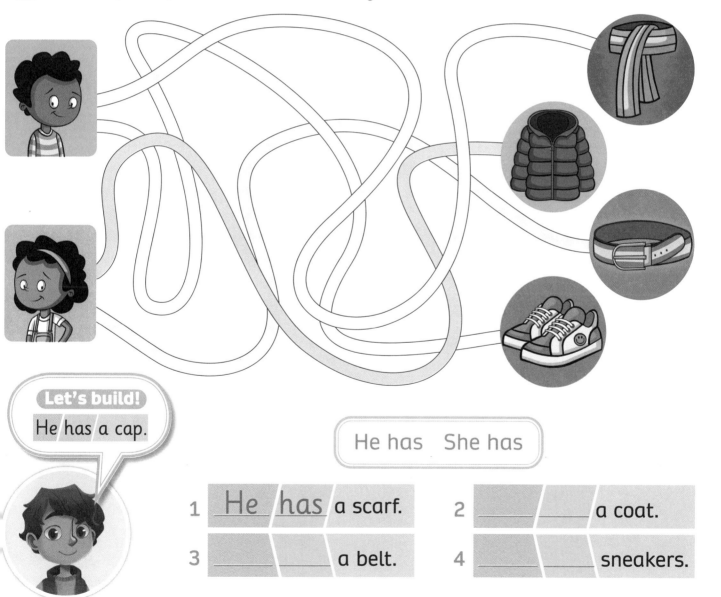

**Let's build!**

He has a cap.

He has   She has

1 He has a scarf.

2 _____ a coat.

3 _____ a belt.

4 _____ sneakers.

Who has long hair in your family? Tell a friend.

**Extra time?**

⑦

**1**  Listen and match.

**My sounds**

**2** 1.14 Listen and repeat. Then circle.

1 ( w ) / y    2 w / y    3 w / y    4 w / y    5 w / y

**I can shine!**

**3** ✏️ Listen to a friend and draw. Then share.

He has a long coat.

She has a dark, red scarf.

color me

**1** Look and write. Then say.

builder   ~~chef~~   explorer   teacher

**1**  **2**  **3**  **4**

*He's a chef.*

chef  _____  _____  _____

## I can shine!

**2** Read and circle. Then role-play.

**Think and share**
What can you say about your friend's picture?

*Look at this!*

*Oh, what a great picture! / This is for you!*

color me

When can you comment on a picture? Tell a friend.

Extra time?

**1** Trace. Then check (✓) or put an ✗ for you.

I have...

1 a backpack. ☐     2 sneakers. ☐

3 glasses. ☐     4 a watch. ☐

5 a scarf. ☐     6 a coat. ☐

7 a belt. ☐     8 a cap. ☐

**2** Look and write.

chef   coat   dark

1 She has _____ hair.

2 She has a white _____.

3 She's a _____ .

**3**  Ask. Then check (✓) or put an ✗ for your friend.

*Do you have...?*

 ☐      ☐      ☐      ☐

He has short, dark hair and a backpack. He's an _ _ _ _ _ _ _ _ _ _ .

**Extra time?**

**4** ✏️ ✂️ 💬 **Stick and color. Then play the game.**

start

finish

*She has a short, green scarf.*

*Different! She has a short, purple scarf.*

**5** **Read. Then think and write.**

## My Things

**I have...**

_____

_____

_____

_____

**I don't have...**

_____

_____

_____

_____

Make a backpack. Then share with your family.

**Home-school link**

# Let's be happy at home

**Let's review!** `SB p10–11` Find and trace. Then say.

coat · belt · cap

**1** Trace and number.

kitchen ☐    bedroom [1]

living room ☐    bathroom ☐

yard ☐    hallway ☐

garage ☐    stairs ☐

**Tell me!**
What can you find in the yard? Circle.

pajamas

tree

flower

footer_page_number 12

Say the words in alphabetical order.    **Extra time?**

**1** (2.06) **Listen and circle.**

**1**

a      b

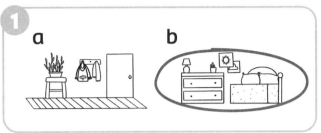

**2**

a      b

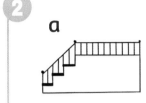 

**3**

a      b

**4**

a      b

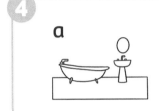 

**2** **Circle and trace. Then look and write.**

### livingroombedroomyard

1 Where's Mom? She's in the _____.

2 Where's Dad? He's in the _____.

3 Where's Grandma? She's in the _____.

**I can shine!** ✳

**3** 💬 **Choose a room and write. Then ask and answer.**

*Where's Peanut?*

*He's in the _____.*

color me

Circle what's in your house: stairs/kitchen/garage. Tell a friend.

Extra time?

**1** SB p22–23 ➡ **Trace. Then read and circle.**

**1**

*He's in the*
bathroom /
kitchen.

**2**

*Clara is in the*
living room /
bedroom.

**3**

*He's in the*
garage /
yard.

**2** **Follow. Then circle.**

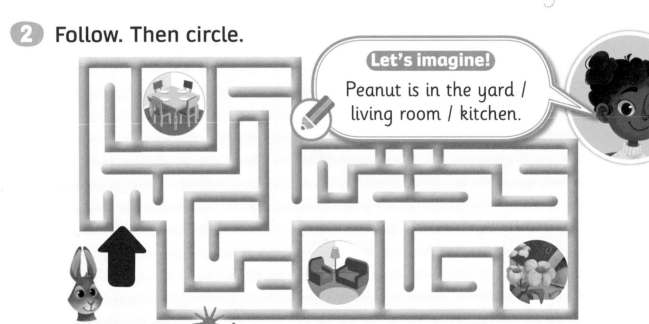

**Let's imagine!**

Peanut is in the yard /
living room / kitchen.

**I can shine!**

**3** **Look at Activity 1. Write and say.**

*Peanut*
_____ _____ _____
_____.

*Oscar is in the*
_____.

*Tess is in*
_____
_____.

color me

14

Which is your favorite story frame? Why? Tell a friend.

**Extra time?**

**1** Read and trace. Then number.

table ① · bed ☐ · couch ☐ · lamp ☐

**2** Read and circle. Then write.

on   next to

**Let's build!**
Where's the book?
It's on the table.

1 Where's the bed / table? It's _____ the couch.

2 Where's the book / lamp? It's _____ the table.

3 Where's the watch / scarf? It's _____ the bed.

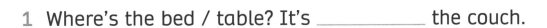
Where's your English book? Tell a friend.

Extra time?

15

**1**  Listen and number.

**My sounds**

**2**  Listen and repeat. Then circle.

**1** r / l   **2** r / l   **3** r / l

**I can shine!**

**3** 🖊️💬 Draw two things. Write. Then ask and answer.

Where's the...?

It's _____
the _____.

color me

**1** Match and write. Then say.

| cave igloo tent ~~tree house~~ |

 **1**  **2**  **3**  **4**

tree house _____ _____ _____

 **a**  **b**  **c**  **d**

It's a tree house.

**I can shine!**

**2** Read and write. Then role-play.

**Think and share**
Do you like your home? Why?

Let's put the T-shirt in the backpack.

color me

What rooms do you clean up at home? Tell a friend.

Extra time?

**1** **Find and circle. Then write.**

| a | b | a | t | h | r | o | o | m | c |
|---|---|---|---|---|---|---|---|---|---|
| l | i | v | i | n | g | r | o | o | m |
| r | o | p | s | t | a | i | r | s | t |
| e | y | a | r | d | o | n | w | y | r |
| o | o | m | g | a | r | a | g | e | d |
| c | y | h | a | l | l | w | a | y | s |
| d | f | g | b | e | d | r | o | o | m |
| i | k | i | t | c | h | e | n | l | g |

**1** bathroom

**2** _____

**3** _____

**4** _____

**5** _____

**6** _____

**7** _____

**8** _____

**2** **Draw and check (✓). Then ask and answer.**

| Where's the...? | | |
|---|---|---|
| on the table | | |
| on the bed | | |
| next to the bed | | |
| next to the lamp | | |

*Where's the...?*

*It's...*

18

It isn't a room. You can go up and down. They're __ __ __ __ __ __ .

Extra time?

**3** ✏️ 🩹 💬 **Stick and color. Then play the game.**

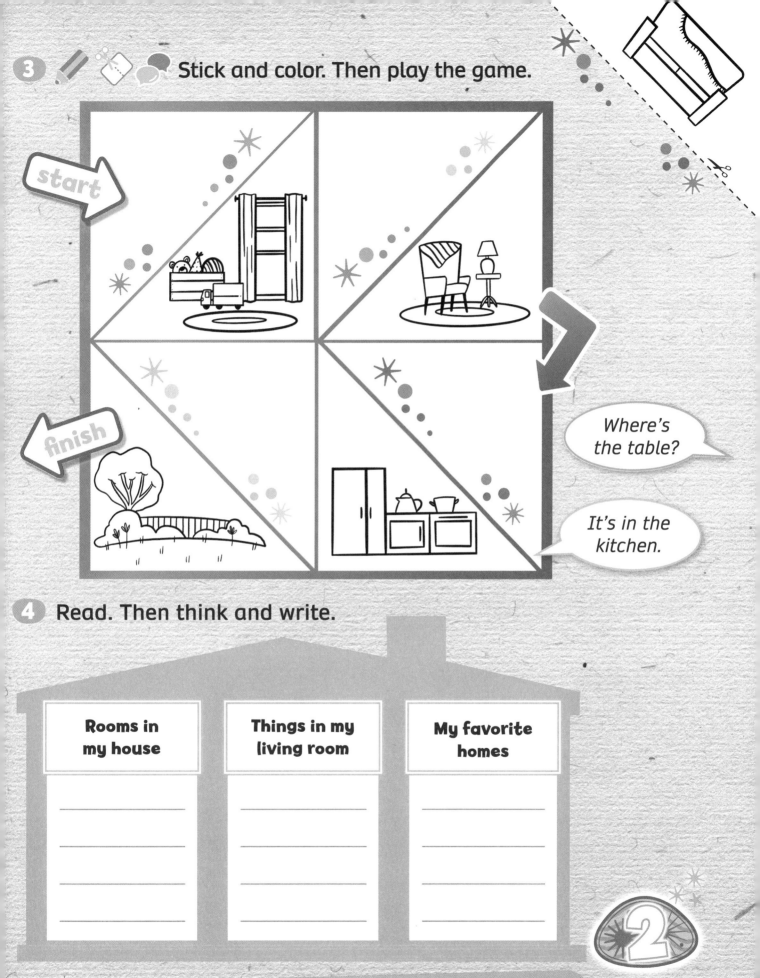

start

finish

Where's the table?

It's in the kitchen.

**4** **Read. Then think and write.**

| Rooms in my house | Things in my living room | My favorite homes |
|---|---|---|
| _____ | _____ | _____ |
| _____ | _____ | _____ |
| _____ | _____ | _____ |
| _____ | _____ | _____ |

Make a tent. Then share with your family.

🏠 Home-school link

2

**1** Read and trace. Then write the letter.

 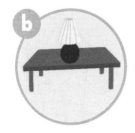  

1 Do you have a backpack? Yes, I do. **d**

2 Where's Mom? She's in the bedroom.

3 He has dark glasses.

4 Where's the lamp? It's on the table.

5 Do you have white sneakers? Yes, I do.

6 Where's Dad? He's in the yard.

7 She has a long scarf.

8 The couch is next to the table.

**2** 2.19 Listen and number. Then say.

  1

## 3 Find and circle six words. Then write.

(Do)haslongoninWhere

1 ___Do___ you have a watch? No, I don't.

2 She has a _____ coat.

3 _____'s Mom?

4 Dad is _____ the kitchen.

5 My brother _____ dark hair.

6 The lamp is _____ the table.

## Mini-project

4 ✏ Draw your friend. Then write and say.

He / She has _____
_____.

What a _____ picture!

## Time to shine! ✳✳

5 ✏ Read, write, and color.

My things and My home

I can read _____ new words.

I can write _____ new words.

I can ask and answer questions about what I have and where things are.

I can sing two new songs.

# 3 Let's explore nature

## Lesson 1 ➡ Vocabulary

**Let's review!** SB p20-21 ➡ Find and trace. Then say.

bathroom  yard  garage

**1** Look and write.

goose  chicken  turkey  goat  sheep  donkey  ~~cow~~  horse

1  COW
2  _____
3  _____
4  _____
5  _____
6  _____
7  _____
8  _____

chicken

donkey

horse

**Tell me!**
Find and circle the one that doesn't belong.

Say the words in alphabetical order.

**Extra Time?**

**1** Listen and check (✓) or put an ✗.

**1**    **2**    **3**    **4**    **5**    **6**

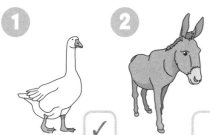    

✓ ☐ ☐ ☐ ☐ ☐

**2** What's at the farm? Trace, color, and write.

There's    There isn't

1 <u>There's</u> a cow.    2 _____ a donkey.

3 _____ a sheep.    4 _____ a goat.

**I can shine!**

**3** Look at Activity 2 and circle *Yes* or *No*. Then say.

*There's a...*

*There isn't a...*

1 There's a white goat.    Yes / No

2 There's a brown horse.    Yes / No

3 There's a brown cow.    Yes / No

color me

Write your favorite farm animal. _____

**Extra Time?**

(23)

**1** SB p34–35 **Look and read. Then write.**

cow   horse   sheep

This is for the

_____ .

Where's the

_____ ?

I can hear a

_____ .

**2** **Look and write.**

chicken   goat   horse

**Let's imagine!**
What food do they like?

1 This is for the _____ .

2 This is for the _____ .

3 This is for the _____ .

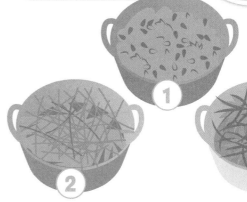

**I can shine!**

**3** **Which animals are at the farm? Write and say.**

There's a _____, a _____, and a _____ at the farm.

color me

24

Which is your favorite story frame? Why? Tell a friend.

Extra time?

**1** Look and write.

bush ~~fence~~ rock wall

1. a _fence_
2. a _____
3. a _____
4. a _____

**2** Follow, find, and write. Then say.

**Let's build!**

There's a horse behind the wall.

1
2
3
4

1 There's a ___goose___ behind the ___rock___.

2 There's a _____ behind the _____.

3 Where's the _____? It's behind the _____.

4 Where's the _____? It's behind the _____.

Who is behind you now? Tell a friend.

Extra Time?

**1** (3.13) Listen and check (✓) or put an ✗. Then match.

**My sounds**

**2** (3.14) Listen and repeat. Then circle.

1   oo / ee

2   oo / ee

3   oo / ee

**I can shine!**

**3** ✏ Write. Then choose, circle, and draw.

's   isn't

There _____ a cow.

There _____ a horse.

It's behind the
wall / fence / bush / rock.

color me

26

**1** Look, read, and circle. Then say.

**1**

hear / (smell)

**2**

taste / see

**3**

hear / smell

**4**

taste / hear

**5**

taste / touch

*I can smell a flower.*

**Think and share**
Close your eyes.
What can you hear?

I can shine! ✴ ★ ✴

**2** Read, circle, and write. Then role-play.

*Excuse _____.*
*_____*
*the park?*

*It's behind the cafe.*

Where's your favorite park? Tell a friend.

**Extra Time?**

**1** Look and write.

Across ➡

**2**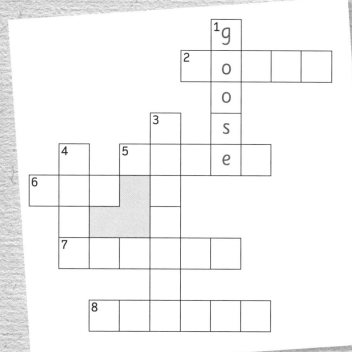

**5**

**6**

**7**

**8**

Down ⬇

**1**

**3**

**4**

**2** Look and read. Then circle.

1  There's a bush.  ✓ / ✗

2  There isn't a wall.  ✓ / ✗

3  There's a donkey.  ✓ / ✗

4  There's a goose behind a fence.  ✓ / ✗

**3**  Look at Activity 2. Play *True* or *False* with a friend.

> There's a goose.

> True!

> It's behind a bush.

> False!

It has two legs. It gives us eggs. What can you hear?

**Extra Time?**

**4** 🖍 ✂️ 💬 **Stick and color. Then play the game.**

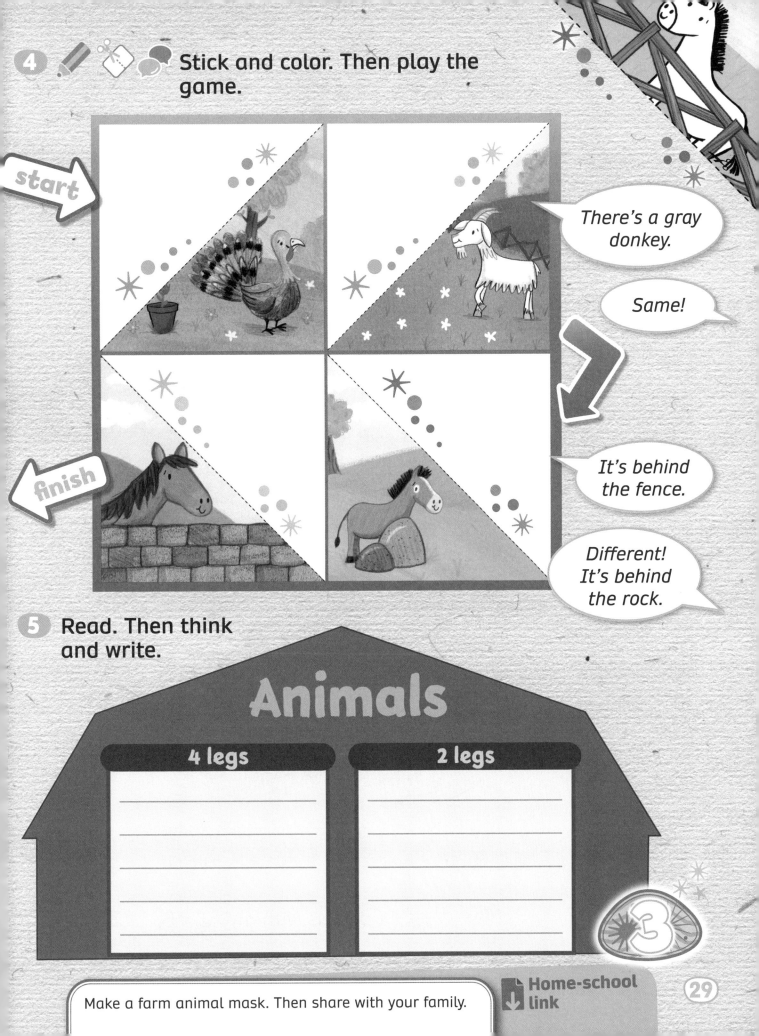

start

There's a gray donkey.

Same!

It's behind the fence.

Different! It's behind the rock.

finish

**5** **Read. Then think and write.**

## Animals

| 4 legs | 2 legs |
|---|---|
| | |
| | |
| | |
| | |
| | |

Make a farm animal mask. Then share with your family.

Home-school link

# Let's try new activities

**Let's review!** SB p32–33 ➡ Find and write. Then say.

_____   _____   _____

**1** Look and write.

kick   swim   catch   roller-skate   ~~jump rope~~   climb   ride   swing

1 <u>jump rope</u>

2 _____

3 _____

4 _____

5 _____

6 _____

7 _____

8 _____

**Tell me!** Think and write.

I do this with my  _____

I do this with my  _____

Say the words in alphabetical order.

**Extra time?**

**1**  Listen and circle.

**1**

a  b

**2**

a  b

**3**

a b

**2** Write. Then follow and circle.

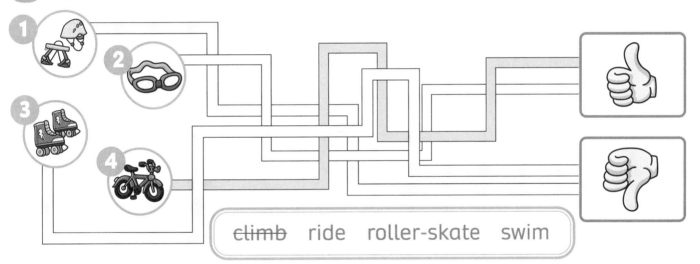

climb  ride  roller-skate  swim

1 Can you  climb ?  Yes, I can. / No, I can't
2 Can you _____?  Yes, I can. / No, I can't.
3 Can you _____?  Yes, I can. / No, I can't.
4 _____ _____ _____ a bike?  Yes, I can. / No, I can't.

Can you swing?

No, I can't. But I can roller-skate!

**3** 💬 Guess the words. Then ask and answer.

sgwni    blcim    lerlor-estak

color me

What can you do? _____

Extra time?

**1** SB 44–45 ➡ **Look and read. Then write.**

| climb   swim   swing |

Can you

_____ , Clara?

Can you

_____ , Tess?

I can

_____ .

**2** **Look and write.**

| climb   roller-skate   swing |

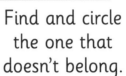
**Let's imagine!**
Find and circle the one that doesn't belong.

_____

_____

_____

**I can shine!**

**3** **Think and write. Then mime and guess with a friend.**

Can you _____ ?

Can you _____ ?

No, I can't.

Yes, I can.

color me

Which is your favorite story frame? Why? Tell a friend.

**Extra time?**

**1** Look and write.    **2** Number. Then circle and write.

a board game   soccer   ~~tennis~~   the guitar

**2** play _____

play tennis _____ **1**

play _____

**3**

**4**

play _____

**Let's build!**
Can he play soccer?
Yes, he can.

**3** Can he / (she) play the guitar?     No, she can't. _____

☐ Can he / she play soccer?     _____

☐ Can he / she play a board game?     _____

☐ Can he / she play tennis?     _____

What can you play? Tell a friend.     Extra time?

**1** 🎧 4.13 Listen and check (✓) or put an x.

|  | 👧 Ann | 👦 Bill |
|---|---|---|
| ride a bike | x |  |
| play soccer |  |  |
| climb |  |  |
| swim |  |  |

**My sounds**

**2** 🎧 4.14 Listen and repeat. Then match.

/eɪ/    /aɪ/

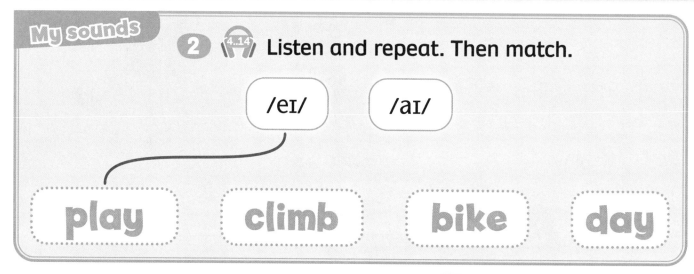

play    climb    bike    day

**I can shine!**

**3** 💬 Think and write. Then ask and answer.

*This is Supergirl.*

*Can she jump rope?*

*No, she can't, but she can play tennis!*

Name: _____
Can: _____
Can't: _____

color me

## 1 Write and number. Then say.

*I can play the recorder.*

| drums | piano | ~~recorder~~ | violin |

 a  b  c **1**  d

 1  2  3  4

recorder _____ _____ _____

## I can shine!

**Think and share**

What can you play with one friend, a lot of friends, or no friends?

## 2 Read, write, and circle. Then role-play.

*Would you like to join my club?*

*Yes, of course! I'd _____ to join your _____.*

Name: _____
Come to my club!
You can _____ and _____!

Answer: Yes, of course. / No, thanks.

*color me*

Which is your favorite club? Tell a friend.

**Extra time?**

**1** **Find and circle. Then write.**

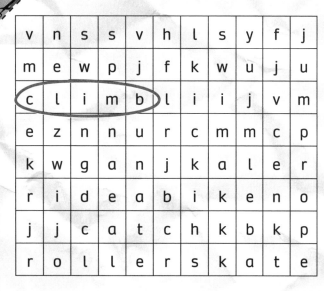

| v | n | s | s | v | h | l | s | y | f | j |
|---|---|---|---|---|---|---|---|---|---|---|
| m | e | w | p | j | f | k | w | u | j | u |
| c | l | i | m | b | l | i | i | j | v | m |
| e | z | n | n | u | r | c | m | m | c | p |
| k | w | g | a | n | j | k | a | l | e | r |
| r | i | d | e | a | b | i | k | e | n | o |
| j | j | c | a | t | c | h | k | b | k | p |
| r | o | l | l | e | r | s | k | a | t | e |

**1** climb       **2** _____

**3** _____       **4** _____

**5** _____       **6** _____

**7** _____       **8** _____

**2** **Look and check (✓) or put an ✗ for you. Then say.**

> *I can kick. But I can't jump rope!*

 ☐    ☐    ☐   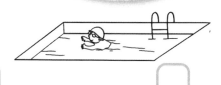 ☐

**3** **Ask and answer. Then circle and write.**

> *Can you play the guitar?*

Friend's name: _____

(He) / She  can play _____ the guitar.

He / She _____ soccer.

> *Yes, I can.*

He / She _____ a board game.

You play it with your mouth. You can hear it. What is it?

**Extra Time?**

**4** ✏️ ✂️ 💬 **Stick and color. Then play the game.**

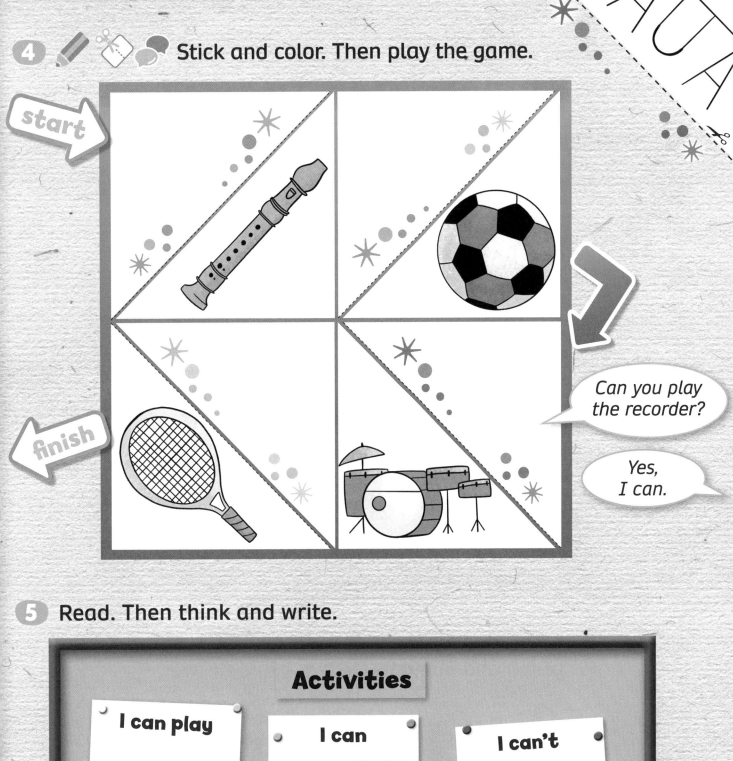

start

finish

Can you play the recorder?

Yes, I can.

**5** **Read. Then think and write.**

### Activities

**I can play**

**I can**

**I can't**

Make a board game. Then share with your family.

Home-school link

# Review 2 All about me

**1** Read and write.

1 Can you <u>roller-skate</u>? No, I can't.

2 There isn't a sheep. There's a _____.

3 She can't jump rope. But she can _____!

4 Can he _____ the guitar? No, he can't.

5 Look! There's a _____!

6 Look! There's a _____!

7 Can you _____? Yes, I can.

8 Where's the _____? It's behind the _____.

**2**   Listen and number. Then ask and answer.

Where's the farm?

It's behind the house.

**3** Guess the words. Then write.

1 Listen! I can _hear_ a cow!

2 Can you _____ a bike?

3 Can he _____ the drums?

4 Look! I can _____ a chicken.

ehra

deri

ylap

ese

  Mini-project

**4** Draw and write. Then ask and answer.

 **Join the Explorers Club!**

You can _____ and
_____.

*Would you like to join the Explorers Club?*

*Yes, of course! I'd like to join your club.*

**Time to shine!**

**5**  Read, write, and color.

**Farm animals and Actions**

I can read ___ new words.

I can write ___ new words.

I can sing two new songs.

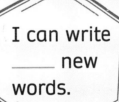 I can ask and answer questions about what there is and things I can do.

# Let's share our food

**Lesson 1 → Vocabulary**

**Let's review!**　SB p42–43　Find and write.
Then say.

_____  _____  _____

**1** **Look and write.**

| orange | burger | fish | juice | ~~egg~~ | cookie | cereal | carrot |

1 _egg_____

2 _____

3 _____

4 _____

5 _____

6 _____

7 _____

8 _____

**Tell me!**
Find and circle
the one that
doesn't belong.

burger　　　orange

juice　　　fish

Say the words in alphabetical order.

**Extra time?**

**1**  **Listen and number.**

 1

**2** **Read, write, and circle.**

1 I'm eating / drinking _____ . euijc

2 I'm eating / drinking a _____ . rubreg

3 I'm eating / drinking _____ . hisf

**3** **Choose and color. Write for you. Then ask and answer.**

What are you doing?

I'm drinking _____ juice.

JUICE

color me

Write your favorite food. _____ Then say *I'm eating...*

**1** `SB p56–57` **Look and read. Then write and number.**

| eating | growing | washing |

 **a**

 **b**

 **c**

Are you _____ my salad, Oscar?

Are you _____ salad leaves, Oscar?

I'm _____ my vegetables!

**2** **Find two words. Then write.**

I'm eating e_____ and _____.

c i g 4 s f s g

**Let's imagine!** What are you eating?

**I can shine!**

**3** 💬 **Mime. Then ask and answer.**

What are you doing?

I'm eating cereal.

color me

Which is your favorite story frame? Why? Tell a friend.

**Extra time?**

**1** **Look and write.**

cook   grow   make   ~~wash~~

wash _____   _____   _____   _____

**2** **Look. Then read and write.**

Nora

Dad

Eva

Remi

**Let's build!**
Are you growing tomatoes?

Yes, I am.   No, I'm not.

1 Are you growing strawberries, Nora? _Yes, I am._

2 Are you making cookies, Eva? _____

3 Are you cooking fish, Dad? _____

4 Are you washing an apple, Remi? _____

Mime an action with a friend. Ask and answer *Are you... ?*

**Extra time?**

**1** 🎧 5.13 **Listen and circle.**

**1** a    b

**2** a    b

**3** a    b

**4** a    b

---

**My sounds**

**2** 🎧 5.14 **Listen and repeat. Then write *i* or *o*.**

**1**  o

**2** ☐

**3** ☐

**4** ☐

**5** ☐

**6** ☐

---

**I can shine!**

**3** 💬 **Choose. Then ask and answer.**

Are you making a sandwich?

No, I'm not.

Are you eating an orange?

Yes, I am.

color me

**1** Look and write. Then say.

| butter | ~~flour~~ |
| fruit | vegetables |

**1**

**2**

*I need flour.*

flour

**3**

_____

**4**

_____

**I can shine!**

**Think and share**

What color are your favorite foods?
Do you like green vegetables?

**2** Read and write. Then role-play.

I _____ fruit for the cake.

OK, let's go _____ !

color me

**Extra time?**

Where do you go shopping? When? Tell a friend.

**1** Look and write.

Across ➡

Down ⬇

3

5

6

8

1

2

4

7

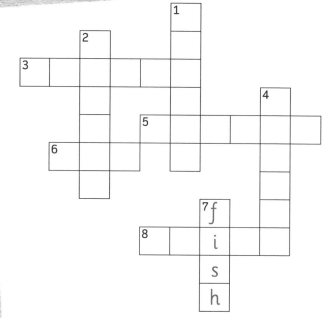

**2** Look and write. Then circle.

1 Are you _____ strawberries?
Yes, I am. / No, I'm not.

2 Are you _____ carrots?
Yes, I am. / No, I'm not.

3 Are you _____ a burger?
Yes, I am. / No, I'm not.

**3** Choose. Then ask and answer.

Orange!

No, I'm not.

Yes, I am.

Are you growing an orange?

Are you eating an orange?

It isn't a fruit. It's an orange vegetable. What is it?

**Extra time?**

**4** Stick and check (✓) or put an ✗. Then ask and answer.

Are you eating a carrot?

Yes, I am.

Are you drinking juice?

No, I'm not.

**5** Read. Then think and write.

# FOOD AND DRINK

At home      At parties      On vacation

_____      _____      _____

_____      _____      _____

_____      _____      _____

Make a paper salad. Then share with your family.

Home-school link

# Let's have vacation fun

**Let's review!** SB p54–55 ➡ Find and write. Then say.

_____ _____ _____

**1** Look and write.

| sleep | ~~vacation~~ | beach | comic books | sandcastle | shells |

**1** go on <u>vacation</u>

**2** build a _____

**3** read _____

**4** _____

**5** collect _____

**6** play at the _____

**Tell me!**
Write *a* for actions and *t* for things.

read [a]  shells [ ]

comic books [ ]  collect [ ]

Say the words in alphabetical order.  Extra time?

**1**  Listen and check (✓).

**1**
a   b  ✓

**2**
a   b

**3**
a  b

**4**
a  b

**2** Follow and find. Then circle.

**1** I want to read comic books / collect shells.

**2** I want to read comic books / collect shells.

## I can shine!

**3** Look and write. **My vacation diary!**

I want to  _____ on Monday.

_____ play at the beach on Tuesday.

_____ on Wednesday.

color me

Do you collect things? What? Tell a friend.

Extra time?

**1** `SB p66–67` Look and read. Then write and number.

~~sandcastle~~   shells   soccer   to   want

*I want to build a*
<u>sandcastle</u>*!*

*I _____ to*
*collect _____!*

*I want _____*
*play _____!*

**2** Read and write for you.

**Let's imagine!**
What do you want
to do on vacation?

I want to
_____
_____.

*I can shine!*

**3** Check (✓) for you.
Then say.

*I want to
read comic books.*

color me

Which is your favorite story frame? Why? Tell a friend.

**Extra
time?**

**1** **Look and write.**

afternoon   evening   ~~morning~~   night

**1** morning   **2** _____   **3** _____   **4** _____

**2** **Number to make sentences. Match. Then answer for you.**

**a**    **b**    **c**  [1]

**1** play tennis [2]
in the morning? [3]
Do you want to [1]

Yes, I do.

**2** read comic books ☐
Do you want to ☐
in the afternoon? ☐

_____

**3** in the evening? ☐
play the guitar ☐
Do you want to ☐

_____

**Let's build!**

Do you want to sleep in the afternoon?

Do you want to sleep in the morning? Tell a friend.

Extra time?

51

**1**   Listen and check (✓) or put an x.
Then ask and answer.

*Do you want to play soccer in the morning?*

*Yes, I do.*

|  | morning | afternoon |
|---|---|---|
| ⚽ |  |  |
| 🎴 |  |  |
| 🥽 |  |  |

### My sounds

**2**  Listen and repeat. Then write *e* or *u*.

1 w_e_t  2 s__n  3 r__n  4 b__d

5 t__ddy bear  6 f__n  7 ladyb__g  8 r__d

### I can shine!

**3** Choose and write.
Then ask and answer.

*Do you want to sleep at night?*

*Yes, I do.*

_____  _____  _____  _____

play     eat     climb

sleep     read     draw

*color me*

What do you want to do in the evening? Tell a friend.

**Extra time?**

**1** **Look and write. Then say.**

*I like the ocean. It's safe.*

dangerous  flag  ~~ocean~~  safe

1  Look at the ocean _____.
   It's _____.

2  Look at the red _____.
   The ocean is _____.

**I can shine!**

**Think and share**
What things can you do on vacation that you can't do at home?

**2** **Read and write for you. Then role-play.**

Dear Max,
I like my vacation! I like the food and my new friends.
I don't like the hot weather.
Look at the picture. I'm swimming in the ocean. It's great!
See you soon, Zoe

Dear _____,
I like my vacation!
I like _____ and
_____.
I don't like _____.
Look at the picture.
I'm _____.
It's _____.
See you soon, _____

_____
_____
_____

color me

Do you speak English on vacation? What can you say?

Extra time?

**1** **Look and write.**

build a sandcastle  ~~collect shells~~  go on vacation
play at the beach  read comic books  sleep

1  collect shells

2  _____

3  _____

4  _____

5  _____

6  _____

**2** **Write and circle for you. Then ask and answer.**

Do  want  you

1  Do you **want** to play soccer in the afternoon?
Yes, I do. / No, I don't.

2  Do _____ want to sleep in the morning?
Yes, I do. / No, I don't.

*Do you want to play soccer in the afternoon?*

3  ____ you want to eat ice cream in the evening?
Yes, I do. / No, I don't.

*Yes, I do.*

4  Do you _____ to read comic books at night?
Yes, I do. / No, I don't.

You build this on the beach. It's yellow. What is it?

**Extra Time?**

**3** Stick and color. Then tell a friend.

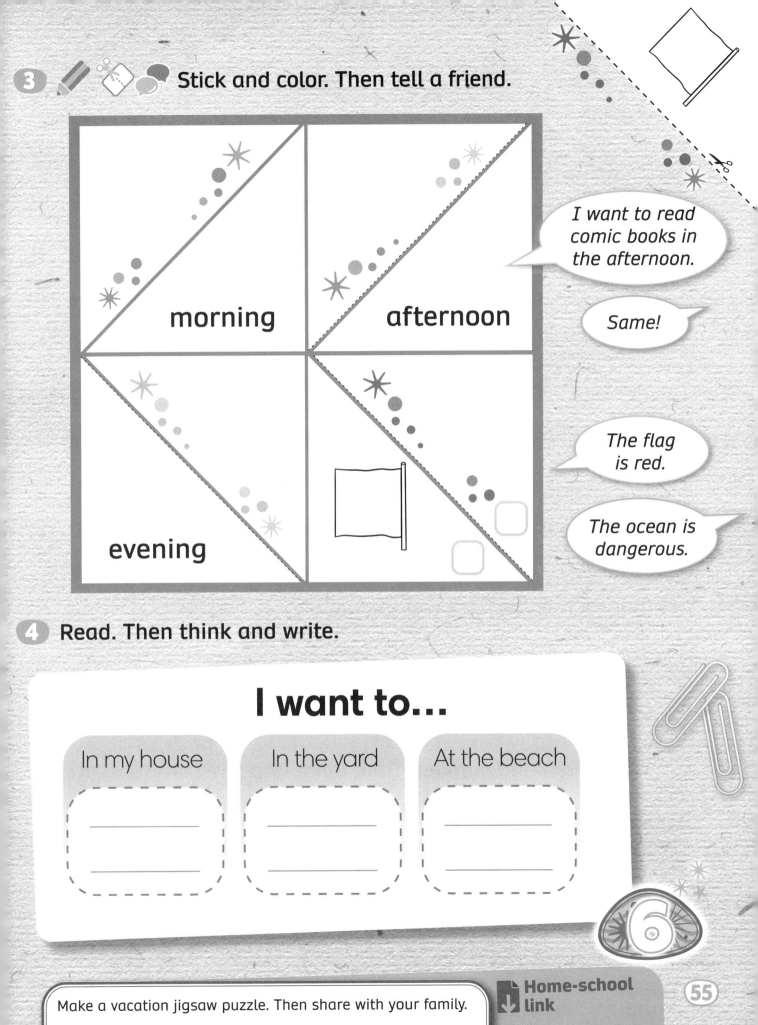

morning

afternoon

evening

*I want to read comic books in the afternoon.*

*Same!*

*The flag is red.*

*The ocean is dangerous.*

**4** Read. Then think and write.

# I want to...

| In my house | In the yard | At the beach |
|---|---|---|
|  |  |  |

Make a vacation jigsaw puzzle. Then share with your family.

Home-school link

# Review 3 — Around me

**1** Look, read, and write.

1 Are you drinking _____? Yes, I am.

2 I want to _____.

3 I'm eating a _____.

4 Do you want to _____ in the afternoon? Yes, I do.

5 I want to _____.

6 I'm _____.

7 I want to _____.

8 Are you eating? No, I'm not. I'm _____ eggs.

**2** (6.19) Listen and number. Then point and say.

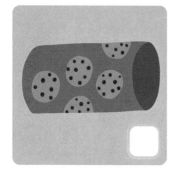

1

## 3 Read and write.

> beach　eating　~~growing~~　vacation

1　Are you _growing_ tomatoes?

2　I want to go on _____!

3　Do you want to play at the _____?

4　I'm _____ cereal.

 **Mini-project**

**4** Draw. Then write and circle.

*Have a great vacation!*

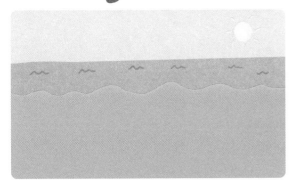

In the morning, I want to

_____.

In the afternoon, I want to

_____.

In the evening, I want to

_____.

I like / don't like my vacation!

**Time to shine!**

**5** Read, write, and color.

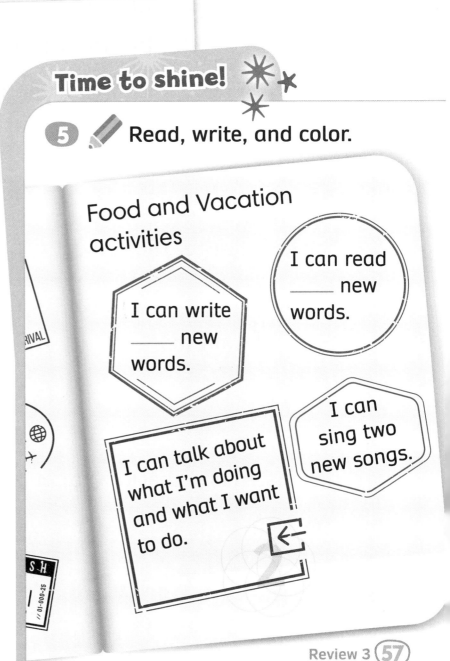

Food and Vacation activities

I can read ____ new words.

I can write ____ new words.

I can talk about what I'm doing and what I want to do.

I can sing two new songs.

# Goodbye from the Explorers Club

**1** **Look and write.**

> build a sandcastle  cap  catch  ~~cook~~  horse
> juice  living room  play the guitar

**1**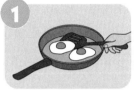

cook

**2**

_____

**3**

_____

**4**

_____

**5**

_____

**6**

_____

**7**

_____

**8**

_____

**2** **Think and write. Then say.**

## I'm an explorer!

| I want to... | I have... |
|---|---|
| _____  _____ | _____  _____ |
| _____  _____ | _____  _____ |

**3** (7.05) **Listen and check (✓) or put an X. Then say.**

 ☒

 ☐

 ☐

 ☐

## 4 Number. Then circle.

This is for the donkey / fish.

Basil, do you want to play tennis / soccer?

My favorite room is the hallway / kitchen.

Can you swim / swing, Clara?

1

Do you have a mascot / rabbit?

What are you growing / cooking?

**Think and share**

My favorite story is in Unit _____ .
My favorite character is _____ .

## 5   Listen and write. Then sing.

explorer   Goodbye   great   Peanut   see

_____, Stella, Tess, and Clara,
Basil, Oscar, and _____, too!
It's vacation time and I'm an _____!
A lot of things to _____ and do!
Goodbye! Goodbye! Have a _____ vacation, too!

# Let them shine!

**1**  **Look and write. Then listen and circle.**

| balloon   barbecue   cake   ~~candle~~   gift   sparkler |
| --- |

  1

  2

  3

candle  _____  _____

  4

  5

  6

_____  _____  _____

*It's your birthday,
let's have fun!
A (cake) and a sparkler
for everyone!
Happy birthday,
happy birthday.
Happy birthday to you!*

# Beautiful world

**2**  **Look and write. Then listen and circle.**

*This is a beautiful world!
How can it be?
Turtles in the (ocean) and
fish in the sea!
Animals on mountains
and hills and in trees!*

| desert   hill
jungle   mountain
ocean   ~~sky~~ |
| --- |

1 sky      2 _____      3 _____

4 _____      5 _____      6 _____

# Amazing oceans

**3** (8.12) **Look and write. Then listen and circle.**

*I can see a (seahorse,)
an octopus, a dolphin,
and a seal!
A shark and a whale –
at the bottom of the
deep blue sea!*

| dolphin   octopus |
| seahorse   seal |
| ~~shark~~   whale |

1 <u>shark</u>    2 _____    3 _____

4 _____    5 _____    6 _____

# Let them fly!

**4** (8.16) **Look and write. Then listen and circle.**

*I'm flying a kite,
I can see the (sun!)
I can see clouds in the sky!
It's day and I'm flying a kite.
Fly, kite, fly!
Fly, kite, fly!*

| cloud   ~~day~~ |
| moon   night |
| stars   sun |

1 <u>day</u>    2 _____    3 _____

4 _____    5 _____    6 _____

# Picture Dictionary

## Welcome

### Vocabulary

| cloudy | rainy | pen | notebook | eraser | ruler |

## Unit 1

### Vocabulary 1

| backpack | belt | cap | coat |

| glasses | scarf | sneakers | watch |

### Vocabulary 2

| dark | blond |

| long | short |

## Unit 2

### Vocabulary 1

| bathroom | bedroom | garage | yard |

| hallway | kitchen | living room | stairs |

### Vocabulary 2

| bed | lamp |

| couch | table |

## Unit 3

### Vocabulary 1

 chicken

 cow

 donkey

 goat

 goose

 horse

 sheep

turkey

### Vocabulary 2

 bush

fence

 rock

 wall

## Unit 4

### Vocabulary 1

 catch

 climb

 kick

 ride

 roller-skate

 jump rope

 swim

 swing

### Vocabulary 2

 board game

 soccer

 guitar

 tennis

## Unit 5

### Vocabulary 1

 cookie

 burger

 carrot

 cereal

 egg

 fish

 juice

 orange

### Vocabulary 2

 cook

 grow

 make

 wash

# Unit 6

## Vocabulary 1

build
a sandcastle

collect shells

go on
vacation

play at
the beach

read comic
books

sleep

## Vocabulary 2

afternoon

evening

morning

night

## Celebration 1

### Vocabulary 1

balloon

barbecue

cake

candle

gift

sparkler

## Celebration 2

### Vocabulary 1

desert

hill

jungle

mountain

ocean

sky

## Celebration 3

### Vocabulary 1

dolphin

octopus

seahorse

seal

shark

whale

## Celebration 4

### Vocabulary 1

cloud

day

moon

night

star

sun